Contents

The vital spark
2

Blowing a fuse
4

All you ever wanted to know about plugs!
6

The striped protector
8

Circuits
10

AC/DC
12

Resistance
14

Varying the resistance
16

Watt a bright idea!
18

Series or parallel?
20

Car electrics
22

Fault finding
24

Behind the wall
26

Burning your money
28

Electromagnetism
30

Electric motors
32

The Vital Spark

Setting the scene

Each year several hundred Europeans are killed by **lightning strikes**. Even people some distance from the strike point may be killed by the very large currents which spread outwards.

When a **thundercloud** passes overhead, large charges are produced in the objects below it (see below left). The cloud then discharges to the ground producing the lightning flash – a giant electric spark. The lightning flash takes less than one millionth of a second and usually (but not always) strikes the highest point.

Tall buildings are protected by using **lightning conductors** (see below right). These are thick strips of copper which run from the top of a building to a metal plate in the ground and conduct lightning safely to earth. They also allow charges at the top of the building to move away towards the cloud, making a strike less likely.

Objects become charged when the number of electrons in an atom changes. The electrons, which are negatively charged, whizz round a positively-charged nucleus. In a **neutral** atom (one with no net positive or negative charge) the number of negative electrons equals the number of positive protons in the nucleus.

If there is a surplus of electrons, the atom becomes negative. If there is a shortage of electrons, the atom becomes positive. When electrons flow from one point to another as in a lightning flash, we say an **electric current** flows.

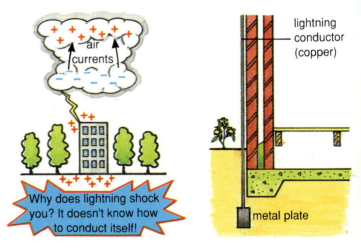

Why does lightning shock you? It doesn't know how to conduct itself!

Insulators and conductors

Electrons do not always stay with their atoms. In an **insulator** the electrons are firmly attached, whereas in a **conductor** the electrons are free to move around and conduct electricity. They are called **free electrons**. Most metals are good conductors while non-metals like plastic, wood and glass are poor conductors (insulators).

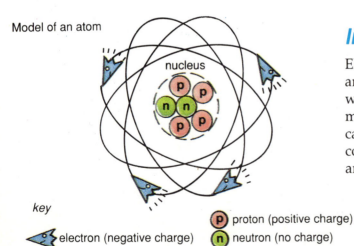

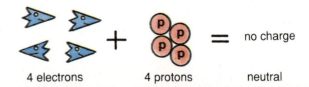

Just good friends | Attraction and repulsion

Protecting aircraft

On average, every civilian aircraft is struck by lightning once a year. Lightning strikes can damage or buckle the thin skin of an aircraft. Look at the photo of the damaged tail fin of a BAe125 aircraft.

Aeroplanes used to be made from **aluminium** – a good conductor of electricity. Nowadays **carbon fibres** and **plastics** are used on areas like the leading edges or the flaps on the wings. These materials are stronger but do not conduct electricity and they have to be coated with a **conducting layer** to prevent serious damage from lightning strikes.

The interior of the plane is not screened. A strike could knock out the modern electronic or electric instruments in the cockpit and elsewhere. This could be disastrous as the pilot relies on these to fly the plane. All the modern electronics have to be screened separately.

DID YOU KNOW?

Basics: voltage and current

Voltage is the electrical push which sends electrons round a circuit. The 'push' is produced by all the electrons trying to get as far away from each other as possible. The bigger the push, the bigger the voltage.

Voltages are measured in **volts** (V).

A **current** is a flow of charges (electrons) round a circuit or wire. The electrons all try to get to the positive side of the battery, but as one arrives, the others push it along. Thus the number of electrons leaving the battery always equals the number arriving back at the battery. None are ever lost on the way round the circuit.

Currents are measured in **amps** (A).

Now try these!

1. What is lightning?
2. Most people struck by lightning could have been saved. How would you start someone's heart beating again?
3. What do similar charges do?
4. What is a current?

5. An atom has five protons and three neutrons. How many charges are in the nucleus and how many electrons are in orbit?
6. Which parts of a modern aircraft have to be screened and why?
7. What is the difference between current and voltage?
8. If the voltage in a circuit increases, what happens to the current flowing?
9. Why must an aeroplane be earthed to the loading gantry when it is refuelled?

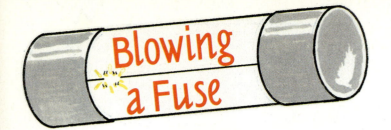

Choosing the right size of fuse can sometimes be difficult. If in doubt, always check the instruction manual or ask an electrician.

To choose the right fuse first of all look at the RATING plate on your appliance.

MODEL DA 14
240 V ~
1400 W
West Germany

Choose the fuse from these recommended sizes:
Up to 700W use a 3A fuse.
Over 700W use a 13A fuse.

Choosing the right fuse

Most domestic appliances convert **electrical energy** into **heat energy**. The rate at which energy is used depends on the **power rating** of the appliance. The higher the rating, the more energy is used in a given time. On the right are some appliances with their rating plates and main energy conversions.

A TV converts electrical energy to light, heat and sound energy

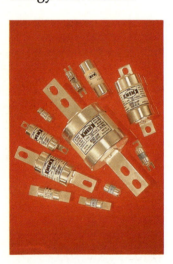

The fuse wire inside the cartridge is made from a tin and lead alloy which melts (or **blows**) when the advised current is exceeded. Fuse wire comes in different thicknesses. In general, the thicker the wire, the more current it allows through. A 3 A fuse wire allows 3 A to flow through it before it blows.

an electric fire converts electrical energy to heat and some light energy

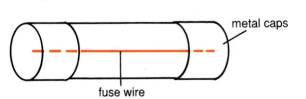

metal caps

fuse wire

A light bulb converts electrical energy to heat and some light energy

Flexes or **cables?**

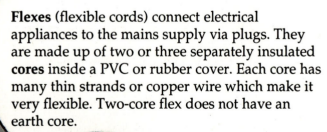

Flexes (flexible cords) connect electrical appliances to the mains supply via plugs. They are made up of two or three separately insulated **cores** inside a PVC or rubber cover. Each core has many thin strands or copper wire which make it very flexible. Two-core flex does not have an earth core.

Cables are used for the fixed wiring around a house. They are not very flexible and would snap if treated like flexes. They carry larger currents than flexes and have to be much thicker. The earth core is not usually insulated as it does not carry any current.

Houses normally have to be rewired every 30 years or so as the insulation deteriorates with age (just like us!).

An Irish company is making mains cables which give off less smoke and toxic gases in a fire. These will have many industrial and domestic uses.

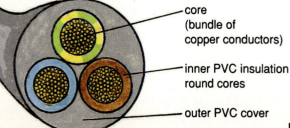

core (bundle of copper conductors)

inner PVC insulation round cores

outer PVC cover

Choosing the right flex

Too large a current flowing through too thin a flex makes it **overheat** and could cause a fire. The table gives the conductor sizes (and suitable fuse sizes) needed for various appliances.

conductor size (area of cross-section) (mm²)	wattage – up to (W)	flex normally used for	maximum current (A)
0.50	750	lamps, hairdryers, hi-fi	3
0.75	1500	fridges, TVs, cleaners	6
1.00	2400 (2.4 kW)	electric drills, kettles, fans	10
1.25	3200 (3.2 kW)	electric fires, extensions	13
1.50	4000 (4 kW)	lighting circuits, storage heaters	16
2.50	7200 (7.2 kW)	sockets, immersion heaters	30
10.00	6000–12000 (6–12 kW)	cookers, instant showers	60

Caution

1. Extension leads should be thick enough for the highest rated appliance used.
2. Extension leads should not be coiled up tightly as they could overheat and melt.
3. Cables running under insulated material may need to be of a higher rating than indicated, as heat cannot escape from the cable.
4. Flexes longer than 2 m should be made of thicker cable.

Multicore cables

DID YOU KNOW?

Flexible compact multicore cables with up to 100 individual cores, which can be easily routed in confined areas, have recently been developed. They use a tough transparent outer cover over a steel wire braid to protect the cables, are water resistant and can withstand temperatures of up to 250 °C.

SHADES

DID YOU KNOW?

Light shades and fittings must be supported by the correct size of flex. Heavy fittings need the extra support of a chain.

cable size	maximum load
0.5 mm²	2 kg
0.75 mm²	3 kg
1.00 mm²	5 kg
chain	over 5 kg

"Why didn't they put it on a chain?"

Now try these!

c 1. What is the difference between a flex and a cable?

2. Which flex size would you use for the following?
   a a 100 W lamp **b** a 600 W drill
   c an electric fire **d** an immersion heater

3. Explain what would happen if you used a 0.5 mm² flex on an electric kettle.

4. Which appliances convert electricity mainly into
   a sound **b** light **c** kinetic energy?

e 5. Describe how a flex is constructed. How does it differ from a cable?

6. What size of flex would you use for a heavy chandelier?

7. Arrange these appliances in order, according to the current needed.

   kettle lamp radio cooker TV drill

8. How do fuses make electrical appliances safer?

ALL YOU EVER WANTED TO KNOW ABOUT PLUGS!

WIRING A PLUG

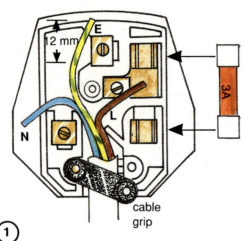

① Strip away outer cover of cable. Unscrew cable grip, insert cable and cut wires 12 mm longer than needed.

② 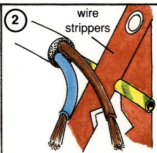 Use wire strippers to cut the insulation 12 mm away from the ends, without damaging the copper wires.

③  Twist the strands of copper wire together to stop fraying.

④ 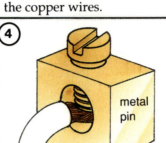 The plastic insulation must stop just before the metal pin.

⑤ 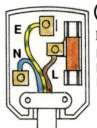 **Remember:**
L = live = brown
N = neutral = blue
E = earth = green and yellow

⑥ The earth pin is longer than the other pins. When the pin is inserted it pushes up a plastic shutter to uncover the live and neutral sockets. This shutter prevents the live from being accidentally touched by children.

⑦ 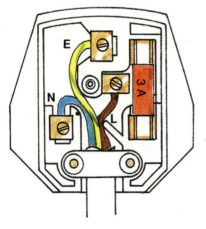 Fit each wire to its correct pin, and tighten the screw securely. Tighten the cable grip.

⑧
IF	THEN
• wires connected to correct pins • no stray strands of wire • cable clamp is secure • all screws tight	• fit the correct fuse • fit the plug cover • collect a Ph D (plug-handling diploma)!

⑨ The cable grip stops the flex being pulled out of the plug. Some plugs have push-fit cable grips into which the cable is pressed.

Do humans conduct electricity?

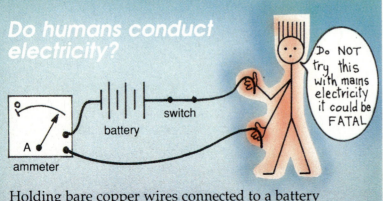

Holding bare copper wires connected to a battery produces a small current. With wet hands the current increases dramatically. Wet skin is a good conductor of electricity, so hands should **always** be dry when touching electrical equipment.

did you know!

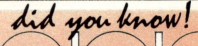

skin, body condition	current through body	effect of current
dry skin, feet on dry insulating surface	small, about 1 mA	shock will give you a bad jolt
wet skin, feet on wet floor, touching metal pipe	large, over 30 mA	electrocution and death ✗

Effect of touching the mains supply. You only need one ✗!

The effect of a current on the heart

The heart muscle stops pumping blood after a serious electric shock. No blood reaches the brain so it is starved of oxygen, and permanent brain damage occurs in a minute or two. Death follows within a few minutes unless the heart is restarted, using artificial resuscitation. **Always take great care when using mains electricity**.

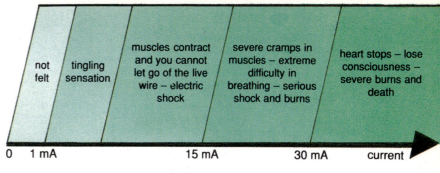

Wiring a coaxial plug

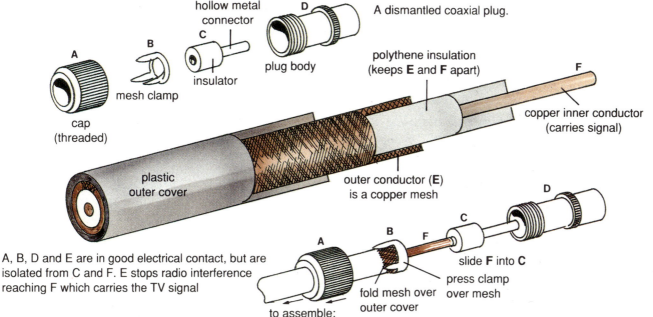

A, B, D and E are in good electrical contact, but are isolated from C and F. E stops radio interference reaching F which carries the TV signal

NOW TRY THESE!

1. Why is electricity more dangerous when your hands are wet?

2. What effect would 20 mA have on your heart?

3. If someone got an electric shock what is the first thing you would do? What would you do next?

4. What is a coaxial plug used for?

5. How many amps in: **a** 1 milliamp (mA), **b** 1 microamp (µA)?

6. How many milliamps in: **a** 0.2 A, **b** 0.02 A, **c** 2.2 A?

7. How many different ways are there of connecting the three wires into the three pins on a plug? How many of these are correct? What is the chance of you getting it correct if you have forgotten the colour codes?
In 'Russian Roulette' using five bullets in the six chambers, what is your chance of picking the right one? Comment on this. Why is wiring a plug wrongly like Russian Roulette?

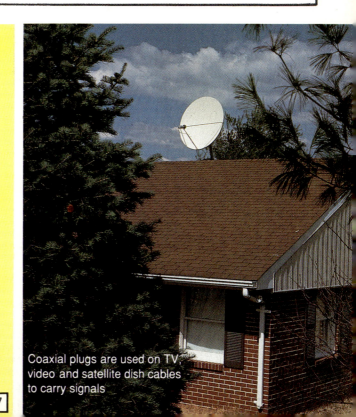

Coaxial plugs are used on TV, video and satellite dish cables to carry signals

The Striped Protector
—THE EARTH WIRE—

The earth wire acts as a safety device. It is the easiest route along which a current can flow to the ground or **earth**. A current will flow along the earth wire in preference to all other paths as it has almost no electrical resistance. If a live wire touches the metal case a very large current instantly flows to earth along the earth wire. This blows the fuse and cuts off the current preventing you from getting a shock or the wires from overheating.

Mrs Sparkie did not know that the earth wire was broken. When she touched the 'live' toaster, enough current flowed through her body to electrocute her. Had the earth wire been complete the fuse would have blown instantly, cutting off the current. Mrs Sparkie should have **unplugged** the toaster before touching it. **Always** unplug an appliance **before** attempting any repairs.

An 'electrician' mixed up the live and neutral wires to a junction box. The electric fire worked for ten years before it got Mr Fry. He **had** switched off the fire but the element was still connected into the live wire. Flash! He had wings!

All electrical equipment that is touched must be earthed and fused correctly. Only when an appliance carries the double insulation symbol – ▣ – does it not need an earth wire, as all the metal parts are insulated with plastic.

Living dangerously

Some basic rules

- Use the **correct size** of fuse. If in doubt ask an electrician.
- Water and electricity don't mix – watch your step if you have **wet hands**.
- Sockets and wall switches in bathrooms can give **fatal** electric shocks.
- **Only** light bulbs should be plugged into light fittings, which have no earth wire.
- **Never** plug more than two appliances into an adaptor at a time.
- Do not join on an extra length of flex to make a longer flex – get an **extension** lead.
- **Check** that flexes are not worn, frayed or cut. Damaged flexes should be replaced.

Is this your house?

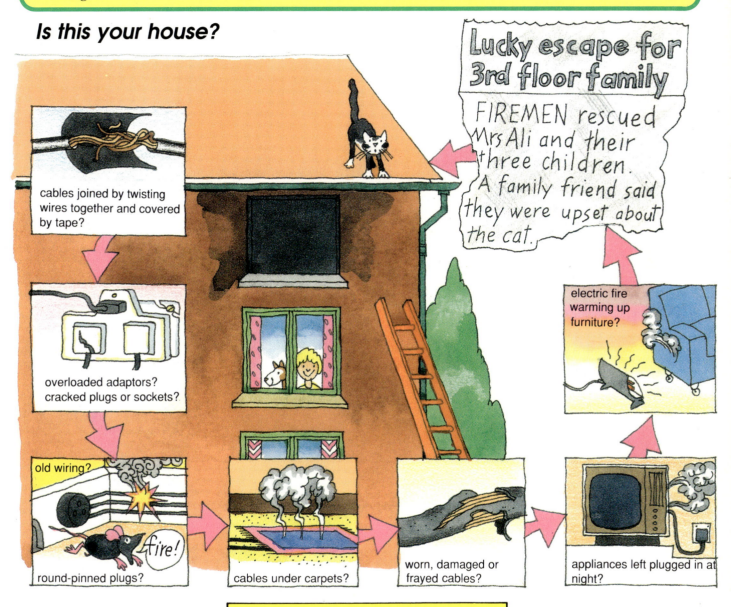

Now Try These!

1. Explain how the earth wire protects you from an electric shock.
2. What should you do with old or worn cables?
3. How do electrical fires start?
4. Why must the fuse and switch be on the live side?
5. Explain why a double insulated appliance needs only two wires.

6. If the live wire of a guitar was connected to the earth terminal by mistake, what would happen to a musician who lifted it up?
7. What might happen if you touched a wet wall light switch?
   What type of switch should you use:
   a in a bathroom, **b** for an outdoor switch?
8. Why must the metal case of an appliance be connected to the earth wire?

Circuits

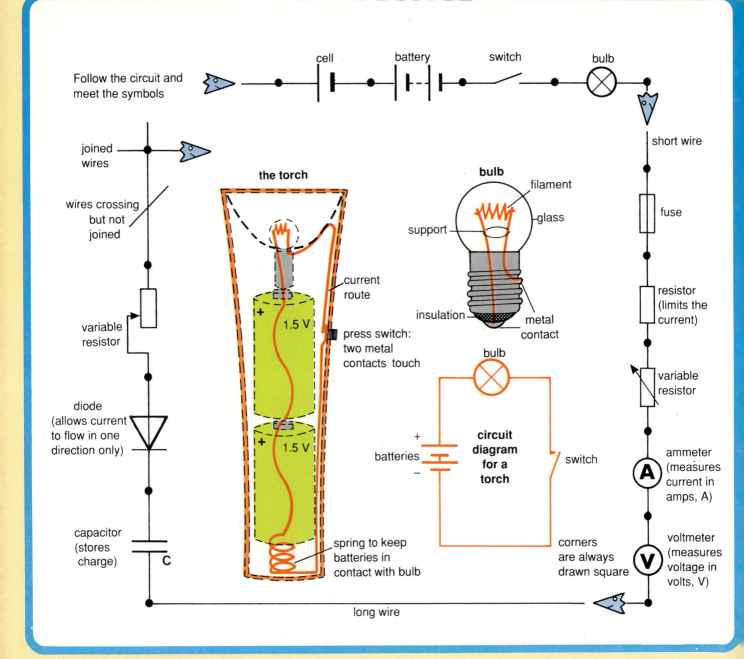

Electric current and charges

When a battery is attached to a conductor, the electrons are attracted to the positive side of the battery. An electric current is caused by a flow of negatively charged electrons. Each electron carries a charge (Q) of 1.6×10^{-19} **coulombs**, so that one coulomb (the unit of charge) is equivalent to about 6×10^{18} electrons.

The connection between current and charge is:

charge = current × time

or $Q = I \times t$

charge in coulombs (C), current in amps (A), time in seconds (s)

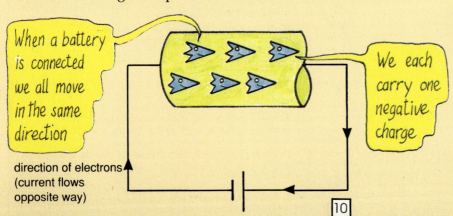

When one coulomb of charge flows along a wire in one second we get a current (I) of one ampere (1 amp; 1 A). So an amp is equivalent to about 6 million million million electrons flowing along a wire in 1 second!

Voltage (or potential difference)

This is the electrical push which forces electrons round a circuit.

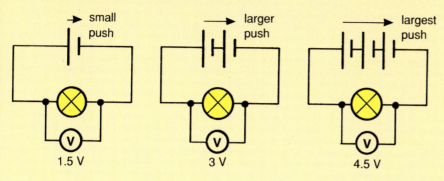

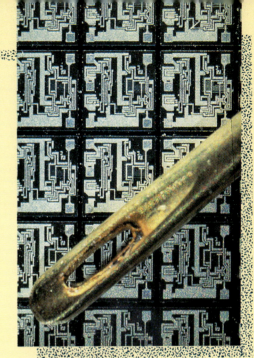

Electrons need energy before they will flow. A voltage of one volt gives one **joule** (J) of energy to each coulomb (C), of charge. A 1.5 V battery gives 1.5 J to each coulomb, whereas a 240 V supply from the mains gives 240 J to each coulomb and is more dangerous.

Modern electronic circuits are microscopically small

As and Vs
Using ammeters and voltmeters

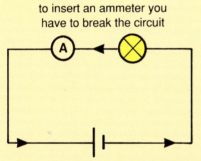

ammeters are always connected **in series** to measure the current flowing through the bulb

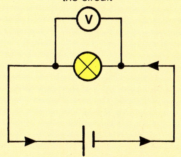

voltmeters are always connected **in parallel** across the components: they measure the voltage **across** the bulb

Electric sticking plaster

Small electric currents can help heal damaged muscle tissues. A new plaster dressing has tiny pieces of copper, zinc and tin (all metals) in the dressing. When they come into contact with sweat from the body, they act like tiny batteries, producing about 30 mV. No one knows how small currents affect cell repair, but 80% of muscle injuries are helped by the new plaster.

now try these!

1. Explain why we use symbols and circuit diagrams to describe circuits.
2. If 180 coulombs pass through a bulb in 1.5 minutes, what is the current?
3. A radio operates on 12 V. How many 1.5 V batteries would you need? How would they be connected?
4. How do you connect a voltmeter to a circuit? How many leads would you use?
5. A battery charger uses 2 A for 6 hours. How much charge flows into the battery? If half the charge flows from the battery in 5.5 minutes, what current flows?
6. Copy and complete this table:

Q	I	t
20 C	4 A	
	1 A	60 s
1000 C		2 minutes
	5 mA	2 s
2 mA		4 minutes

AC/DC

Symbols
-o+ -o- DC supply   ∿ AC
-o∿o- AC supply   -(N)- CRO

DID YOU KNOW?

Battery or mains?

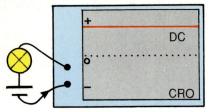
with DC the current flows in one direction from negative to positive

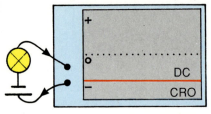
the current flows to the CRO in the opposite direction but it is still DC (− to +)

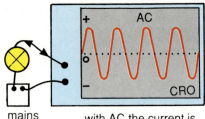
mains transformer — with AC the current is changing direction all the time

After a normal battery (which provides **direct current**, DC) is used it is thrown away. It is a very expensive way of storing electricity. Using a cassette player for only 20 hours will cost about £1 for batteries. If you use mains electricity (**alternating current**, AC), you will get 30 hours of listening for 6 p (the price of a unit of electricity). In general, the smaller the battery, the more expensive the electricity.

The other advantage of AC over DC is that the voltage can be altered using transformers. (See page 12 of *Physics Now! – Energy*.) This is not easy with DC.

AC mains

The mains supply is alternating current, AC. It changes its direction one hundred times every second. One positive (+) and one negative (−) part are called a **cycle**. Mains produces 50 cycles each second, and so has a frequency of 50 hertz (50 Hz). The current flows for 0.01 s in one direction and then 0.01 s in the opposite direction, then 0.01 s in the first direction, and so on...

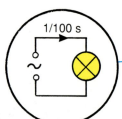

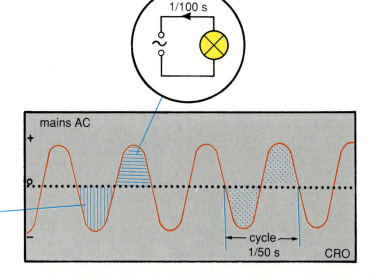

RMS

Mains voltage is quoted as 240 V AC. This is equivalent to the DC voltage which would produce the same heating or lighting effect. In fact, the AC voltage changes all the time – from 340 V to 0 V and back to 340 V during each cycle. This averages out at 240 volts over the cycle. It is called the **root mean square** (RMS) value of 240 V.

So 340 V peak is equivalent (in power) to 240 V (RMS) AC.

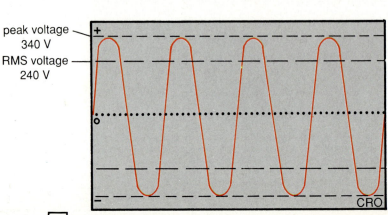
peak voltage 340 V
RMS voltage 240 V

Effects of AC/DC

It makes no difference to lamps, heating elements or resistors whether they run from AC or DC; the same heating or lighting effect is produced. For capacitors, which are used to store charges, and diodes, there is a difference.

Capacitors	Diodes
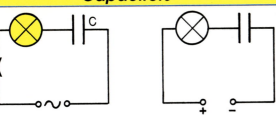	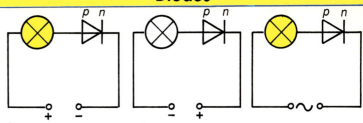
Only the AC circuit works. Capacitors block DC, i.e. they do not let it through.	The diode only conducts in one direction, when the p-side is positive. On AC the bulb lights but is dimmer, as the diode only conducts half the wave (half wave rectification).

Are fields dangerous?

DID YOU KNOW?

Controversy still surrounds reports that electromagnetic fields from power lines could be responsible for some childhood leukaemias. Studies in the USA have shown that very weak alternating magnetic fields from cookers or electric blankets can have biological effects. This unexpected result has prompted a doubling of the research budget in this field to £1 million!

METER WITH A SWING!

DID YOU KNOW?

A new range of digital meters costing over £0.5 million to design and build uses a **liquid crystal display** (LCD) to show a pointer moving across a traditional analogue scale. These old-fashioned displays are very easy to read, but just in case some of you have difficulty in telling where the big hand is, the designers have included a modern, very accurate digital readout as well!

Microprocessors control the new meters and if you touch something with more than 20 volts, a buzzer sounds a warning.

The instrument's case has been designed to withstand being dropped 6000 times from 1 m onto concrete, so it should last at least a week with the electricity board's engineers.

Now try these!

 1. List ten appliances which use mains electricity. For each example discuss how the job would have been done in the last century before electricity was generally available.

2. What is the difference in the electricity from a battery and that from a transformer?

3. What is the frequency and voltage of the mains?

 4. Is 340 V the peak voltage or the RMS voltage?

5. All meters measure RMS voltage. Why is this?

6. If the RMS value is 0.7071 × peak value, what would the RMS values be for these voltages?
   a 240 V peak   **b** 340 V peak

7. Describe the effects of AC on capacitors and diodes.

In 1827 Georg Ohm discovered that if a conductor was kept at a steady temperature then the ratio of voltage to current was constant. He found that if the voltage across a conductor was doubled or tripled, then the current increased accordingly. When the same voltage from a battery is applied across different conductors it produces different currents. This led him to the idea of **resistance**, where a conductor tries to stop or **resist** a current. The conductor which has the least current flowing through it has the highest resistance, or opposition, to the current; its ratio of V/I is highest.

Resistance is measured by the ratio V/I, where

$V/I = R$ (resistance)

This is called **Ohm's law** (see page from notebook).
  Ohm's reward for discovering his law was to get the sack from his teaching job!

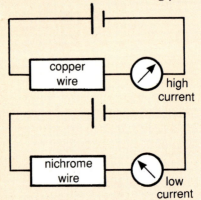

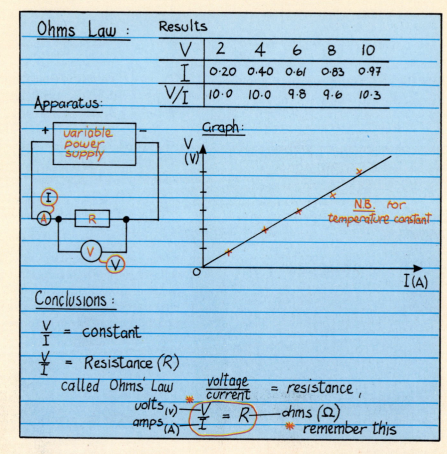

A **resistor** is a component which tries to stop a current from flowing.

A bigger voltage is needed to push the same size current through a material which has a higher resistance. Here are the values of some resistors.

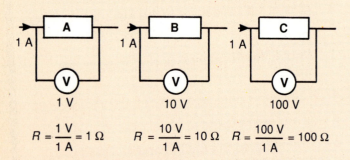

resistor **C** has the highest resistance

Non-ohmic conductors

Some materials like semiconductors and gases do not really obey Ohm's law. They are called non-ohmic conductors. How their voltage and current vary is more complicated.
  Your body is a non-ohmic conductor. This table shows how your resistance varies with the voltage applied.

voltage (V)	current (A)	resistance (Ω)
60	0.025	2400
120	0.060	2000
240	0.250	1000

Free electrons

We're not attached to any particular atom!

Free electrons are electrons not strongly bound to their atoms. The current flowing in a conductor depends on the number of free electrons that are available. When these enter a material of high resistance, they are held up by the atoms in the materials and this causes resistance. Plastics resist the motion of electrons strongly. Their resistance is one thousand million million million times that of copper! In plastics and other insulators the electrons are firmly bound to the atoms.

Uses for resistors

- **In circuits** resistors control voltages and currents, allowing other components like transistors to work correctly.
- **In heating elements** the wire used has a high resistance so that most of the electrical energy carried by the electrons is converted into heat.

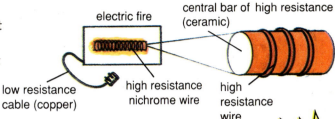

electric fire — low resistance cable (copper) — high resistance nichrome wire — central bar of high resistance (ceramic) — high resistance wire

Superconductors Heat Up

Superconductivity was discovered in 1911 by the Dutch scientist Heinke Onnes. He found that mercury cooled to –269 °C lost its resistance. Superconductor materials cooled below their **critical temperature** conduct electricity without changing it into heat. They offer the possibility of transmitting electricity with no loss. Below the critical temperature they also exclude magnetic fields so that a magnet will float above a superconducting material (see photo).

Until 1986 expensive liquid hydrogen and helium were used to cool superconductors below their critical temperatures. Since then scientists discovered that copper oxide ceramics containing **rare earth metals** only needed to be cooled to –173 °C before they became superconducting. To reach this temperature, cheap, safe, plentiful liquid nitrogen (boiling point –196 °C) can be used for cooling.

These new **high temperature superconducting materials** will dramatically cut the cost of running body scanners which use expensive liquid helium. They could also be used to make super-fast computers, trains that float over magnetic rails, and have many other applications.

Resistance won't disappear overnight; after all, lamps, cookers, electric fires and immersion heaters still rely on it to produce heat.

Magnet floating on superconductor ▷

DID YOU KNOW?

Now Try These!

1. What is the name given to the opposition which an electron experiences when moving through a conductor?
2. List the symbols used for current, voltage and resistance. How are they connected?
3. Draw a circuit to measure the resistance of a lamp at different currents.
4. What are superconductors? Why have they become more viable?
5. Explain what happens to a current when a resistor is added.
6. What do these mean? **a** 60 kΩ **b** 0.5 MΩ
7. What current flows round the circuit? If the resistor were replaced by a lead of low resistance (0.1 Ω) what current would flow and how would it affect the wire?

4 V, 12 Ω

8. Copy and complete this table.

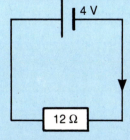

V	I	R
25 V	5 A	
2 V	10 A	
	12 A	6 Ω
3 mV	6 mA	
100 kV		50 Ω

VARYING THE RESISTANCE

Resistors which change their resistance are called **variable resistors**.

Variable resistors have many uses. Here are two.

1 Volume control

Linear type
Moving the slider from A to B decreases the amount of wire in the circuit and hence the resistance between XY; this increases the current and the **volume** from the loudspeakers.

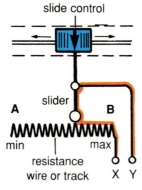

Rotary type
Rotary variable resistors use a curved carbon track or fine resistance wire. A knob controls the position of the contact and hence the current flowing in a circuit. They are used in controls for TVs and radios.

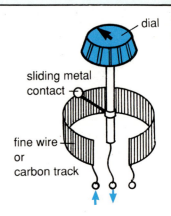

2 Model car controller

The more current that flows into the electric motor in the car, the faster it goes. The amount of current is controlled by a variable resistor in the **handset**. When the trigger is squeezed gently, the sliding contact (or **wiper**) moves to B. Here only a small current flows to the car as most of the resistance wire is in the circuit. Squeezing the trigger more firmly moves the contact to C, where there is less resistance wire in the circuit. The current is increased and so the speed of the car increases.

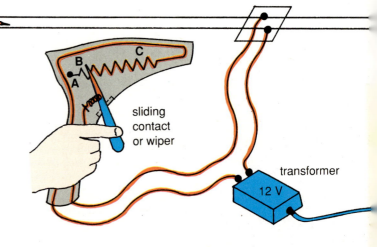

Talking electrons

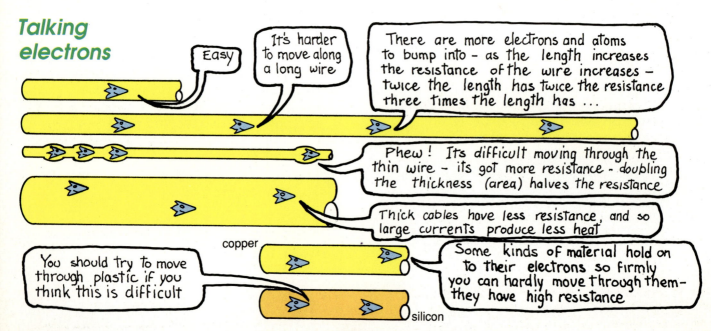

The lie detector

When you tell a lie your heart beats faster. More blood is pumped to the skin, which quickly becomes moist. Its resistance is decreased almost immediately. Scientists have made use of this phenomenon in developing the lie detector.

A suspect is attached to the lie detector machine by **electrodes**. If he or she does not answer a question truthfully the change in the resistance of the skin is detected by the machine and gives a visual or audible warning to the detective.

Conducting plastics

Plastics have recently been developed which have low resistances like metals. When their low weight is taken into account, they now rival metals for many applications. A German company is already using conducting plastics in a new lightweight battery.

Resistance and temperature

Apart from a few special alloys, the resistance of most materials changes as the temperature varies. As the temperature increases most metals increase their resistance, except for semiconductors which decrease their resistance.

1 Metals

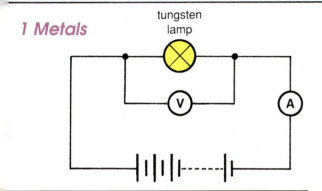

As the temperature rises, the **temperature** of the **filament** and its **resistance** increase. At high temperatures the tungsten atoms vibrate more, causing more resistance.

A cold 60 W light bulb has a resistance of about 100 Ω so that at switch on the current flowing is 2.4 A (from $V = IR$; 240 = $I \times 100$). When lit, the filament (at 2500 °C) has a resistance of 1000 Ω, and takes only 0.24 A (from $V = IR$; 240 = $I \times 1000$). The fuse chosen, normally 3 A, must cope with the **overload current** at switch on if it is not to blow. Old bulbs usually burn out when they are switched on, due to this overload current.

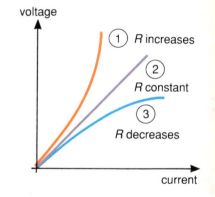

① R increases
② R constant
③ R decreases

2 Alloys

Special alloys, like constantan, which always have the same resistance are used in some circuits to cancel out the effects of temperature changes.

3 Semiconductors, thermistors

As the temperature rises, the number of free electrons rises and so the resistance falls. Thermistors are used to limit the overload current produced when a TV is switched on.

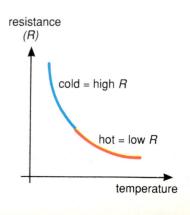

cold = high R
hot = low R

Now try these!

1. Explain how a variable resistor works.
2. Explain how a lie detector works.
3. To make the volume louder, do you increase or decrease the resistance in a circuit? How do you change the resistance?
4. What might happen if you used a lawnmower with a 200 metre cable?
5. A 1 km cable of area of cross-section 10 mm² has a resistance of 1.6 Ω. Find the resistance of
   a. a 100 m length of this cable,
   b. a 50 km length of this cable,
   c. a 1 km length of the same cable but with an area of cross-section of 1 mm².
6. Plot a graph of resistance against temperature for these thermistor results.

V/V	120	120	120	120	120	120	120	120
I	12.2 mA	32 mA	75 mA	160 mA	0.32 A	0.60 A	1 A	1.7 A
T/°C	0	20	40	60	80	100	120	140

What would be the temperature of the thermistor when its resistance was 2.5 kΩ?
Estimate its resistance at: **a** 150 °C, **b** −20 °C.

WATT A BRIGHT IDEA!

Edison tried various materials for filaments. He even obtained a hair from a Scotsman's beard which he carbonized to make a carbon filament for one of his early lamps! Until tungsten arrived in 1906, carbon was used for filaments as it withstood the high temperature needed to produce light.

In an electric fire, the flex has a low resistance and the element has a high resistance. The same current flows through each so that I^2 is the same for each. Because the heat produced depends on the resistance R, the element, which has a high resistance, gets hot while the cable, with a low resistance, remains cold.

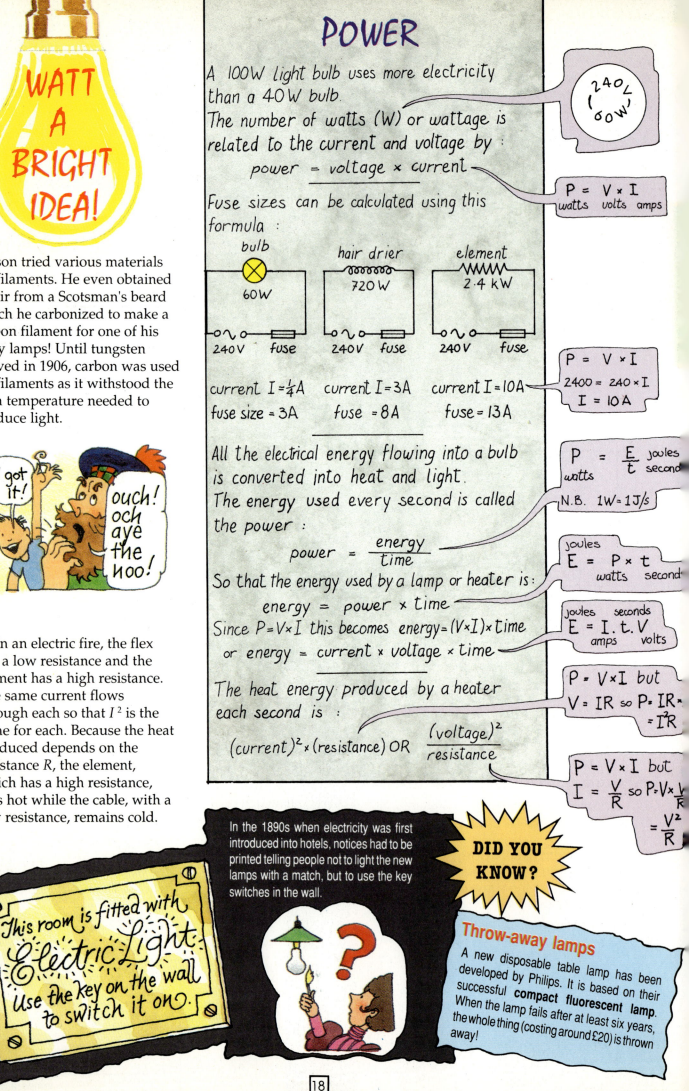

POWER

A 100W light bulb uses more electricity than a 40W bulb.

The number of watts (W) or wattage is related to the current and voltage by:

$$\text{power} = \text{voltage} \times \text{current}$$

Fuse sizes can be calculated using this formula:

- bulb: 60W, 240V, current $I = \tfrac{1}{4}$A, fuse size = 3A
- hair drier: 720W, 240V, current $I = 3$A, fuse = 8A
- element: 2.4 kW, 240V, current $I = 10$A, fuse = 13A

All the electrical energy flowing into a bulb is converted into heat and light. The energy used every second is called the power:

$$\text{power} = \frac{\text{energy}}{\text{time}}$$

So that the energy used by a lamp or heater is:

$$\text{energy} = \text{power} \times \text{time}$$

Since $P = V \times I$ this becomes energy = $(V \times I) \times$ time

or energy = current × voltage × time

The heat energy produced by a heater each second is:

$$(\text{current})^2 \times (\text{resistance}) \quad \text{OR} \quad \frac{(\text{voltage})^2}{\text{resistance}}$$

Side notes:
- 240V, 60W
- $P = V \times I$ (watts, volts, amps)
- $P = V \times I$; $2400 = 240 \times I$; $I = 10$A
- $P = \dfrac{E}{t}$ (watts = joules/second). N.B. 1W = 1 J/s
- $E = P \times t$ (joules = watts × seconds)
- $E = I \cdot t \cdot V$ (joules = amps × seconds × volts)
- $P = V \times I$ but $V = IR$ so $P = IR \cdot I = I^2R$
- $P = V \times I$ but $I = \dfrac{V}{R}$ so $P = V \times \dfrac{V}{R} = \dfrac{V^2}{R}$

In the 1890s when electricity was first introduced into hotels, notices had to be printed telling people not to light the new lamps with a match, but to use the key switches in the wall.

This room is fitted with Electric Light. Use the key on the wall to switch it on.

DID YOU KNOW?

Throw-away lamps
A new disposable table lamp has been developed by Philips. It is based on their successful **compact fluorescent lamp**. When the lamp fails after at least six years, the whole thing (costing around £20) is thrown away!

1 Filament lamps

Modern filaments are made of **tungsten wire**, which becomes very hot (2500 °C) and gives out white light. The lamp is filled with **argon gas** which does not react with tungsten; it also reduces evaporation of the tungsten filament, so prolonging its life. To improve light output, a 1.2 metre length of tungsten wire is coiled and then re-coiled to make a coiled coil (cc) filament. Only about 10% of the energy used a bulb is given out as light; the rest is wasted as heat.

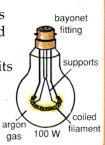

Less glare

Glare produced by floodlights at sportsgrounds may be a thing of the past. Smaller and lighter floodlamps have been developed which are more efficient, so fewer lamps are needed. Light from these **halide** lamps is precisely beamed onto the pitch, doubling the illumination, while drastically reducing the amount of glare produced outside the stadium – and all for a 20% reduction in the electricity used.

Lamps

DID YOU KNOW?

Cooking by light

The latest cookers use **halogen** (quartz-iodine) lamps rated at 1.5 or 1.8 kW to produce the same heat as old-fashioned rings. Pans are placed on a glass surface which is easily cleaned and is an electrical insulator, which is safer. There is no time delay as the heat is produced or controlled instantly.

2 Fluorescent lamps

Mercury vapour at low pressure conducts electricity (i.e. it allows electrons to flow). These electrons collide with mercury molecules which give off invisible **ultraviolet light** (UV). The UV strikes a **phosphor** coating on the inside of the tube and gives out white light (**fluorescence**). Up to 40% of the energy supplied to a tube turns into light. Because they are more efficient, lower wattage tubes can be used to give the same amount of light. The phosphors used in the tubes can cause serious blood-poisoning if they get into a cut.

NOW TRY THESE!

1. List five examples of domestic appliances which change electrical energy into heat energy.

2. A light bulb produces 10 W of light. What size of bulb is it?

3. Why is argon gas used in bulbs?

4. Calculate the fuse size needed for these appliances when connected to the mains.
   a 40 W bulb   **b** 2 kW fire   **c** 300 W TV
   d 750 W vacuum cleaner

5. How much energy do these use in an hour?
   a 40 W bulb   **b** 2 kW fire   **c** 10 W radio
   d 6 kW shower

6. Find the resistance of a 720 W mains drill.

7. An element of resistance 10 Ω draws a current of 12 A. What is its power, and what is the voltage of the supply?

8. Fluorescent lamps have lower wattages for the same light output. Explain this.

9. Copy and complete this table.

P	V	I	R
	2 V	6 A	
	50 V		10 Ω
120 W	10 V		
2 kW		8 A	
50 W			5 kΩ
0.2 MW	25 kV		

Heating

Heating elements

Elements convert all the electrical energy into heat energy. They have a high resistance and use up all the energy carried by the electrons.

The elements of fires, kettles and irons all use **nichrome wire** as it does not oxidize when red hot (900 °C).

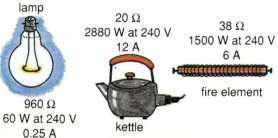

lamp
960 Ω
60 W at 240 V
0.25 A

20 Ω
2880 W at 240 V
12 A
kettle

38 Ω
1500 W at 240 V
6 A
fire element

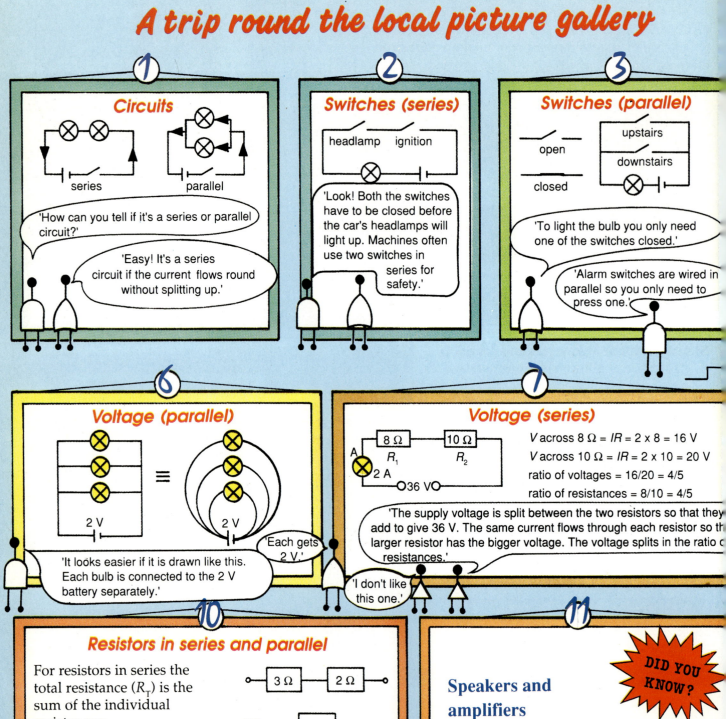

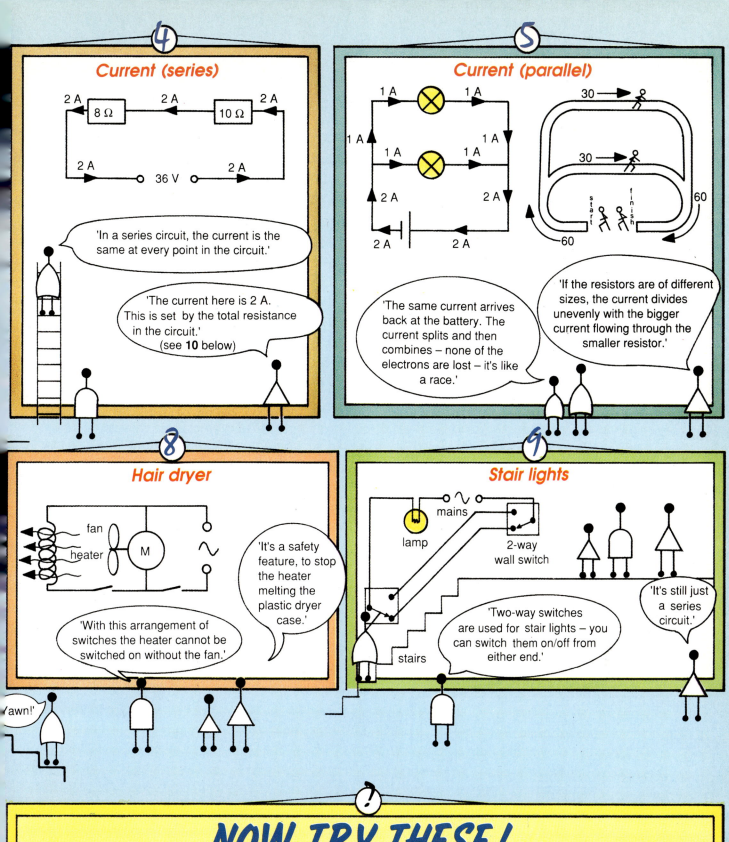

NOW TRY THESE!

1. Explain the main difference between series and parallel circuits.

2. What happens to:
   a. the current when bulbs are added in series,
   b. the voltage when bulbs are added in parallel?

3. Explain why many machines use two switches in series.

4. In a parallel circuit, what is the connection between the total current and the separate currents?

5. Calculate the combined resistance of these resistors in
   a series, b parallel.
   i $2\,\Omega, 4\,\Omega$ ii $20\,\Omega, 20\,\Omega$ iii $1\,k\Omega, 1\,\Omega$
   iv $1\,M\Omega$ and $1\,\Omega$

CAR ELECTRICS

Here are some car circuits.

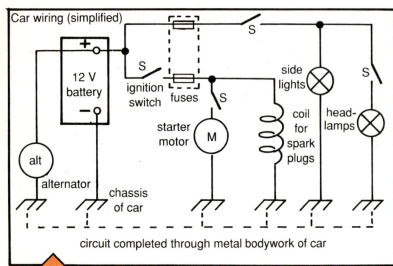

The dotted line shows how the circuits are completed through the metal bodywork of the car. The **chassis symbol** indicates where a circuit is electrically joined to the metal of the car. The bodywork acts as a return wire.

All appliances in a car are connected in parallel so that they all get 12 V from the battery. Notice that the ignition switch **and** another switch have to be closed before an appliance will work.

This shows the completed **side-light circuit** after the switch is closed. Notice the current flows through the bodywork.

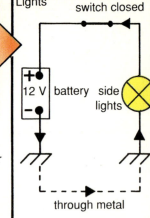

DID YOU KNOW?

CAR BREAKDOWNS

Each year nearly 3 million car breakdowns are caused by electrical faults. More cars use engine management systems, which may be affected by dampness moving along the wire bundles to the connections and terminals.

BMW are introducing a heat-shrinkable cable sleeve with hot-melt adhesive lining. When the sleeve is heated, it shrinks onto the cables; the adhesive melts, sealing any gaps between them, stopping water entering any joints and terminals.

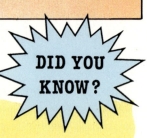

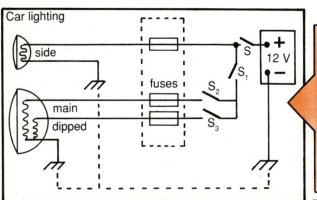

All the lamps are connected in parallel (each gets 12 V). Switches S_2 and S_3 are usually incorporated in a **two-position switch**, so that when S_3 is closed S_2 is open. This prevents main and dipped beams being on at the same time.

A **relay switch** is used to complete the starter motor circuit. This circuit uses very thick wire because up to 60 A may be drawn from the battery when the starter motor is turned.

DID YOU KNOW?

HALOGEN LAMPS

Tungsten halogen lamps used in car headlamps are 50% brighter and last up to three times longer than ordinary filament lamps. They were developed from the quartz-iodide lamps used in cine projectors. Iodine is used instead of argon gas as it stops the tungsten filament from evaporating. Quartz glass is used because iodine vapour reacts with ordinary glass.

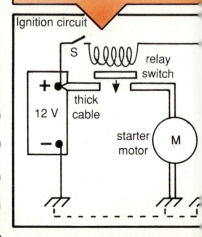

AUTOGUIDE

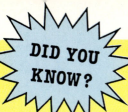

Engineers are working on an automatic car navigation system called **Autoguide**. It is hoped the new system will reduce congestion, travelling times, fuel consumption and save hundreds of lives each year. Roadside beacons fixed to traffic lights transmit a local map and data about traffic conditions to a computer in your car using **infra-red** beams.

A synthesized computer voice tells you which way to turn at junctions and also displays the best route through the traffic on a dashboard display. Horizontal bars at the side of the screen disappear as you approach a turn. All you have to do is type in the postcode of your destination and the central computer which controls the entire operation will do the rest.

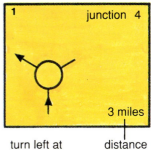

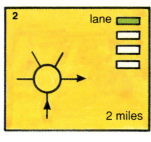

Dashboard display

turn left at junction 4 — distance to turn

at roundabout take 4th exit and 1st lane

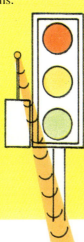

You have been robbed — Stop thief!

The **alternator** (generator) produces all the electricity for the lights etc. when the car is moving **and** has enough left to recharge the battery. The battery supplies the energy for the starter motor and parking lights when the car has stopped.

Computer take-over

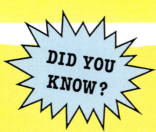

Japanese engineers have developed an automatic speed control for cars. A radar transmitter/receiver measures the distance to the car in front and a central computer keeps your car a safe distance behind it. If the car in front slows down and stops, so do you! The computer also works out the best fuel and air mixture for the driving conditions and reduces exhaust emissions to a minimum. It also controls the headlamps, automatically dipping when oncoming vehicles approach you. All you have to do is steer, and the computer might even do that for you soon!

NOW TRY THESE!

c 1 A 12 V car battery has six cells. What is the voltage of each?

2 Explain how 'Autoguide' works.

3 Why are fuses needed in car wiring circuits even though they are only 12 V?

e 4 Draw circuit diagrams to show:
   a how the switches for the courtesy light in a two-door car are connected,
   b where a horn would be connected.

5 A starter motor takes 60 A. Find its resistance and comment on the thickness of the wire needed.

6 The radio works on 9 V. What size of resistor R is needed if the current is 0.1 A?

FAULT FINDING

Indian satellite fails after one week
Daily Splurge 29 July 1988

A short circuit occurred in one of the power supply lines in the Indian communication/broadcasting satellite 'Inset 1c' which was built by Ford Aerospace. As a result, half of the channels do not work. Regional programmes to local communities in their own languages on topics like hygiene, family planning and teacher training have been severely disrupted.

Faults in electrical or electronic equipment can have serious effects. Checking circuits for faults can be done in several ways.

Continuity tester

Equipment can be tested to see if it is conducting properly by passing a current through it then checking it on an ammeter.

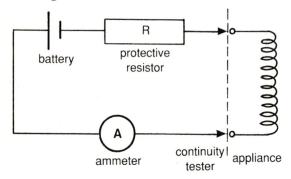

Continuity test circuit

If a current flows the circuit is complete. If no current flows then there must be a break in the circuit. A protective resistor prevents the ammeter from damage if the ends of the leads touch together.

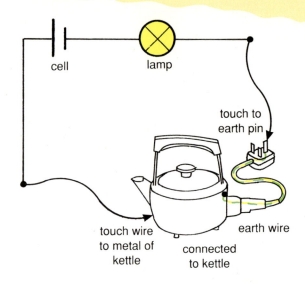

Above is a simpler circuit which only needs a bulb and a battery. It is used to check earth connections. If the lamp is bright, there is a good electrical connection between the earth wire and the metal casing of the kettle. No light or a dim bulb means a poor, possibly dangerous circuit.

Circuit testers should not be used on equipment still connected to the mains!

EMI

Electromagnetic interference (EMI) can cause malfunctions in microprocessor-based equipment like computers, electronic instruments and visual display units. EMI can cause a whole system to fail (**crash**); memories can be destroyed or altered and even the hardware can be damaged.
EMI is produced by various sources.

Lightning

If a power line is struck by lightning, very high surge voltages, or **spikes** (over 100 kV) can damage microprocessor equipment plugged into the mains supply. If a building is struck by lightning, several thousand amps can flow to earth via the metal structure, causing chaos to equipment. Office buildings may need to be equipped with several low resistance (under 1 Ω) conductors for protection.

Electrostatic discharge

Even walking across synthetic carpets in a dry atmosphere can 'charge you up' to 16 kV and can cause problems with computers and data stores.

Radio interference

Radar, CB, radio and other transmitters can affect electronic circuits.

Others

Fluorescent lamps, motors, generators and welders all produce EMI.

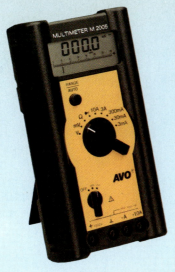

Ohmmeters

Ohmmeters measure the resistance between any two points. The resistance becomes extremely large (MΩ) if the circuit has a break. A short circuit is indicated by a low resistance of nearly 0 Ω. Here are some practical situations.

This multimeter can be used as an ohmmeter

Symbol

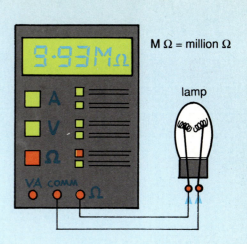

MΩ = million Ω

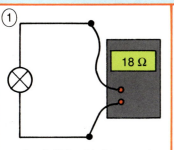

1. circuit OK – this is normal resistance of bulb

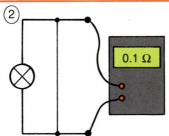

2. bulb short-circuited – meter reads resistance of wire

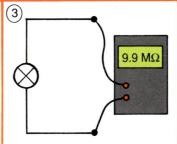

3. high resistance – bulb open-circuited as filament broken

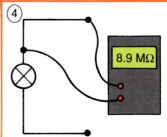

4. wire open-circuited – broken wire – high resistance

Computer systems don't like surges or power failures

UPS

The power supply to a computer must remain absolutely steady to prevent valuable data being lost or changed. **Uninterruptible power supplies** (UPS) provide battery power if the mains fails and, more important, they stop any voltage surges caused by EMI. About half of computer 'downtime' is due to disturbances in the power supply.

Now Try These!

1. Explain how to use a continuity tester.
2. Suggest why a protective resistor is needed in a continuity tester.
3. What is: **a** UPS, **b** EMI, **c** an ohm?
4. Spot the faults in these circuits, and explain them.

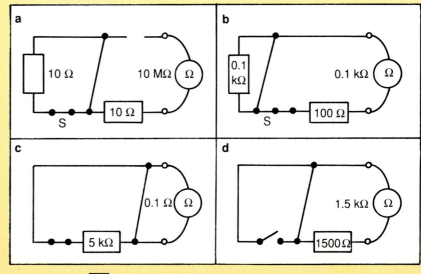

BEHIND THE WALL

Mains supply

Most of the wiring in your home is hidden.

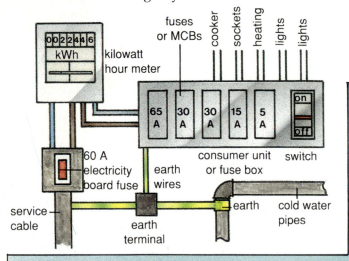

Consumer unit

The earth terminal connects the service cable earth and the consumer unit earth wires to an earthing spike driven into the ground. In the past, they were connected to the cold water pipe, near the stopcock. When a fault develops, a current flows down the spike or water pipe into the ground, and returns to the power station through the soil. This connection must have a resistance of less than one ohm so that it is a **very** good conductor.

The mains supply is 240 V alternating current (AC). It enters your house through a service cable and is connected to your meter via the electricity board's main fuse box, which is sealed. A cable runs from the meter to the consumer unit where the supply is split into several domestic circuits. Each circuit is protected by a fuse or **miniature circuit breaker** (MCB).

Earthing

DID YOU KNOW?

More stringent earthing regulations for houses mean that all houses built before 1986 now have substandard earthing installations. The earthing circuits in your house will soon have to be upgraded, and at your own expense!

Ring mains

The **ring circuit** or **ring main** is a closed loop or ring of three core cable (live, earth and neutral) which connects the sockets in a house. All the sockets are connected in parallel, so that if an appliance is plugged in it gets 240 V from the mains, without affecting the supply to other electrical appliances. Each ring circuit is protected by a 30 A fuse (or MCB).

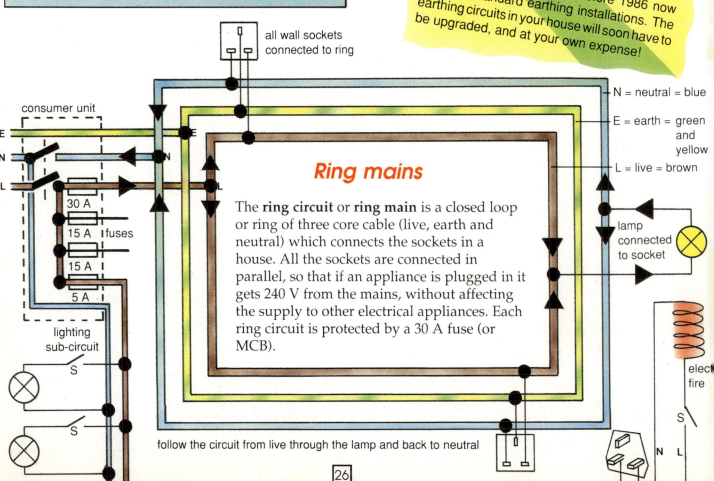

follow the circuit from live through the lamp and back to neutral

Advantages of a ring main

Current can reach any socket by two routes. To supply 30 A, each route carries only 15 A so that much thinner cable can be used which reduces the cost of the circuit. A lower current also produces less heat in the cables.

A single ring circuit can supply many sockets round the house.

Sockets, plugs, fuses etc. are of a standard size and design and so costs are reduced.

Lighting circuits

The lighting circuit in a house is not a ring circuit and has no earth wire. A single cable runs from the consumer unit to several joint boxes around the house. Lamps and switches are connected to each joint box in parallel.

The current used by all the lights together will not exceed 5 A, so thinner wire can be used. A 5 A fuse protects the circuit.

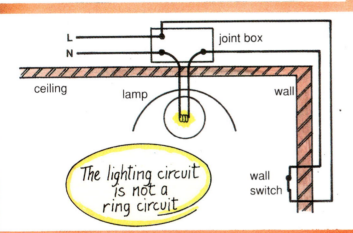

MCBs

Miniature circuit breakers (MCBs) protect circuits from current overload. They are replacing traditional fuses as they **trip** or switch off as soon as a slight overload occurs. A normal fuse may not blow for several hours on a slight overload. After the fault has been corrected, or a faulty appliance unplugged, the MCB is reset by pressing in a button.

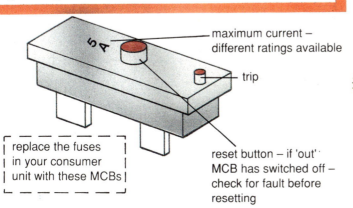

RCDs

A **residual current device** (RCD) switches off the electricity to equipment if it detects a leakage of current to earth. This protects you from electric shock if you cut through your lawnmower cable or accidentally touch a live wire or equipment case. A 30 mA RCD compares the size of the current in the live and neutral wires. Normally these are the same, but if they differ by more than 30 mA the RCD trips the supply. Various ratings of RCD are available. RCDs are sometimes called **earth leakage circuit breakers** (ELCBs).

Warning!
Always unplug an appliance before looking for faults. **Never** touch a damaged flex until it is unplugged.

Now try these!

1. Why is a ring circuit used for the sockets in a house?
2. Why is it not necessary to have a ring circuit for lighting?
3. Explain what the consumer unit does.
4. Fuses are now replaced by MCBs. What advantages do MCBs have?
5. With which electrical appliances should you use an RCD?
6. Explain why appliances like cookers are wired separately.
7. A ring main has a 3.2 kW heater, a 2.6 kW kettle, ten 60 W lamps and an 800 W vacuum cleaner all connected to it. What current flows along each side of the ring?
8. Why are mains voltages generally either 110 V or 240 V and not 12 V? (**Hint** – think power!)

Burning your Money

Electrical energy can be measured very accurately using a meter, and sold to you, the **consumer**.

All the electricity you use passes through the meter in your house where it rotates an aluminium disc. Each turn of the disc is recorded by the counter, which gives the number of **kilowatt-hours** (kWh) or units used.

The number of units used depends on two things:

1 The power rating of an appliance

This is the number of kilowatts used by the appliance. A 1 kW (1000 W) heater uses ten times as much energy as a 100 W lamp does in the same time.

2 The time for which it is switched on

A heater switched on for one hour uses twice as much energy as it would in half an hour. The longer an appliance is used, the more energy is consumed.

if the rating is given in watts, divide by 1000 to give kW

number of units = power rating of appliance x time used
(kWh)   (kW)   (hours, h)

e.g. for 1.5 kW heater used for 4 hours,
number of units = 1.5 x 4 = 6 units

each unit costs 6p

to find the number of units used multiply these together

Energy in a unit (1 kWh)

There are 3 600 000 J of energy in a kilowatt-hour. This is how it is calculated

energy (J) = power (W) x time (s)

There are 1000 watts in 1 kW and 3600 s in one hour.

$E = P \times T = 1000\ W \times 3600\ s$
$E = 3\ 600\ 000\ J$

Because this is such a large number, we do not use joules for electricity bills. Each unit of electrical energy on your bill is a **kilowatt-hour**.
Remember, the kWh is a unit of **energy**, not power.

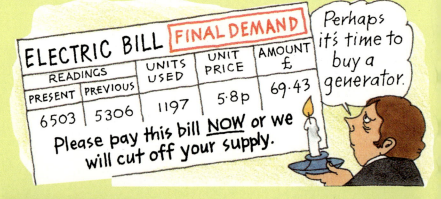

Costs

Domestic appliances convert electrical energy at different rates, and so cost varying amounts to run. Each unit (kWh) costs about 6 p. This is how long things will run for on one unit.

To find out how long an appliance takes to use 1 unit use this...

No. of kW × time = 1 kWh
(÷ W by 1000)

for a 40 W lamp:
$\frac{40}{1000} \times t = 1$, so $t = \underline{25 \text{ hours}}$

for a 6 kW instant shower
$6 \times t = 1$, so $t = \frac{1}{6}$ hour
or $\underline{10 \text{ mins}}$!

and all for 1 unit.

Taking the steam out of your bills!

A new immersion heater should save the average family over £70 per year on its electric bills. The heater has two elements. A long element uses 'cheap' off-peak electricity (Economy-7), for overnight storage, and a shorter element gives daytime 'boosts'. Accurate thermostats measure the temperature of the water in the tank and a controller keeps this temperature constant. In a traditional water heater, the thermostat is set higher than necessary to warm the tank because the element is too short. Nearly 5 million households in the UK use immersion heaters.

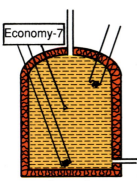

hot tank

White meters

Used for storage heating or water heating, these provide up to seven hours (Economy-7) of night-time electricity at less than half the standard price. Power stations have spare capacity at night and white meters were introduced as a way of increasing the demand. Daytime electricity from these meters is slightly more expensive.

DID YOU KNOW?

Now try these!

c

1. What does a kWh meter measure?

2. How much energy is produced by a 2 kW bar fire in **a** 1 second, **b** 1 minute, **c** 1 hour?

3. To make a pot of tea, a 2 kW electric kettle is on for three minutes. At 6 p per unit, how much does it cost to make:
   a four pots each day,
   b four pots a day for a week,
   c four pots per day for a year?

4. Electricity costs 6 p per kWh. Find the cost of using:
   a a 3 kW fire for eight hours,
   b a 2 kW kettle for three minutes,
   c a 60 W lamp for 12 hours,
   d a 6 W radio for four weeks continuously.

e

5. A 3 kW immersion heater takes one hour to heat enough water for a bath. A 6 kW shower heater is on for five minutes for a shower. Calculate the cost of **a** a bath, **b** a shower. Compare your answers.

6. A 1500 W fridge costs 12 p per day to run. For how long is the compressor on each day?

7. You go on holiday for ten days and accidentally leave a 2 kW panel heater switched **on**. How much does this cost?

ELECTROMAGNETISM

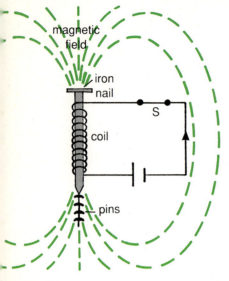

Electromagnets

These are temporary magnets which are **only** magnetic as long as a current is flowing through them. A coil of wire is wound round a **soft iron bar**. When a current flows through the wire, the bar becomes magnetic, but as soon as the current stops, the bar loses its magnetism. 'Hard' magnetic materials like steel become permanently magnetized and cannot be switched off.

Powerful electromagnets have large currents and many turns of wire in the coil.

Uses

Electromagnets have many uses.
- In a steelworks they are used to lift large sheets of steel without bending them.
- At a scrap merchant's, only the **ferrous metals** (iron and steel) are attracted to the electromagnet. Expensive copper and brass are left behind.
- Electromagnets are used in bells, relays, burglar alarms and electric motors.
- They are even used in hospitals to remove metal splinters from your eyes!

The bell

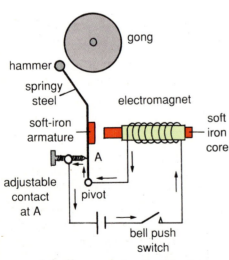

A bell converts **electrical energy** into **sound energy** by using an electromagnet and a simple circuit.

Electrical energy → kinetic energy → sound energy

Symbol

1
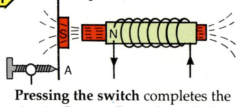

Pressing the switch completes the circuit. Current flows through the electromagnet, magnetizing the armature and iron core with opposite poles, so that they attract.

2
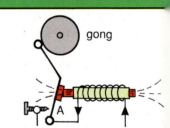

The **armature** is pulled over and the hammer strikes the gong! The circuit is broken at A.

3
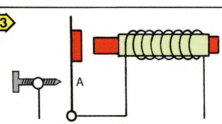

The current stops flowing when the circuit breaks at A. The electromagnet loses its magnetism and releases the armature, which springs back.

4
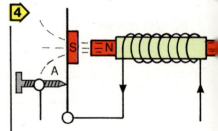

The circuit is complete when contact is made at A. The process is repeated until the button is released.

Door chimes

When the button is pressed current flows through the electromagnet. This attracts the soft iron bar and makes the striker hit the 'ding!' plate. Releasing the button stops this attraction and the spring fires the striker across to hit the 'dong!' plate.

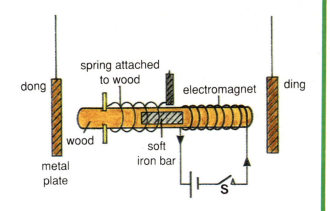

Relays

These are electromagnetic switches which use a small current flowing in an electromagnet to attract an armature. This pivots a shaped iron bar and closes the contacts in another circuit, which may carry a higher current. Relays are used for switching in electronic and electrical circuits. Your fridge has a relay operated by a thermostat, which switches the motor on and off.

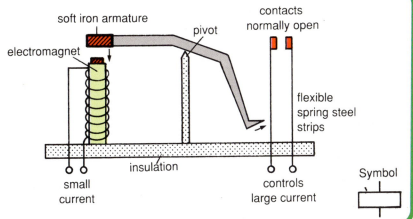

DID YOU KNOW?

Magnetic switches (reed switches)
In a **normally open** (NO) switch, the thin iron strips or reeds are unmagnetized. A permanent magnet closes these by magnetizing the reeds as shown. **Normally closed** (NC) switches have their contacts held open by a magnet.

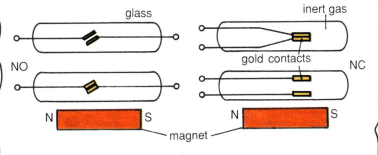

Burglar alarms
When a magnet in a door or window moves away from the reed switch in the frame the reed closes. This energizes the coil in the relay, which switches on the main siren or alarm bell.

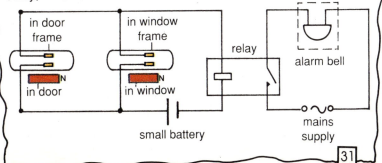

NOW TRY THESE!

1. Explain how an electric current can produce a temporary magnetic field.
2. Explain how an electromagnet works.
3. Explain how the starter motor of a car could be switched on using a relay.
4. List five uses for electromagnets.
5. Why must the contacts of a relay be made of springy metal?
6. Explain how a relay can be used to 'isolate' two different supplies.
7. Why must electromagnets be made from insulated wire? What is used for the insulation? Why is soft iron used for the core?
8. Draw a circuit which uses an electromagnet, a battery and a switch to hold and release a steel ball bearing.
9. Design a burglar alarm system for your house and draw the circuit for it.

ELECTRIC MOTORS

Motor effect

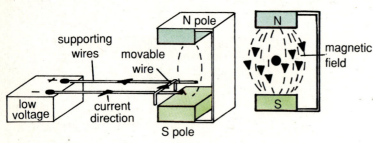

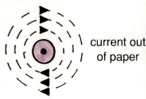

magnetic fields around conductors carrying current: concentric field with no poles

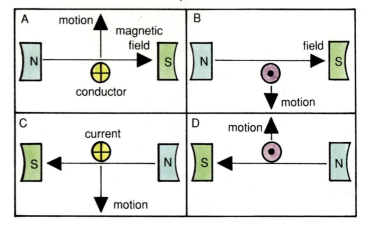

If an electric current is combined with a magnetic field motion occurs. This is known as the **motor effect**. The direction of motion depends on the direction of the current and the magnetic field.

In A, the current is 'into the paper' and the magnetic field is from north to south, to produce an **upward** movement of the conductor. Notice that the current, field and motion are at right angles to each other. The concentric magnetic field produced by a current in a wire is shown here; this interacts with the other magnetic fields to produce motion.

Direction of magnetic field is north to south.

The electric motor

Use the diagrams above to find the motion of the coil.

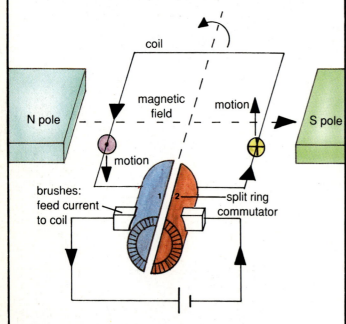

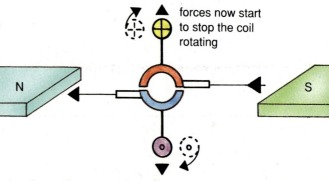

As the coil approaches the vertical, the current is still flowing in the same direction as in 1 (*into* red - *out of* blue). When it passes the vertical, the forces on the coil will slow it down as they are acting in a **clockwise** direction.

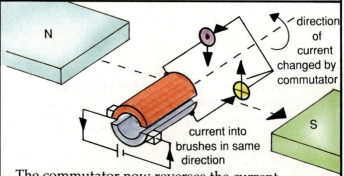

When a current flows through the coil, forces act on the two sides as shown to make the coil turn anticlockwise. The ends of the coil are attached to a **commutator**, a metal cylinder which is split into two halves. Current enters the coil via contacts called **brushes** which press on the commutator. (Current enters the red side and leaves from the blue side.)

The commutator now reverses the current direction. Current enters the blue side and leaves the red side. The forces on the coil continue to turn it in an **anticlockwise** direction. The commutator automatically reverses the current's direction every half turn and keeps the coil rotating anticlockwise.